KNARESBOROUGH
HISTORY TOUR

By the same author:
Harrogate History Tour
Secret Knaresborough
Secret Harrogate
Harrogate Pubs (Including Knaresborough)
Harrogate Through Time
Knaresborough Through Time

First published 2017

Amberley Publishing
The Hill, Stroud,
Gloucestershire, GL5 4EP
www.amberley-books.com

Copyright © Paul Chrystal, 2017
Map contains Ordnance Survey data
© Crown copyright and database right
[2017]

The right of Paul Chrystal to be
identified as the Author of this work
has been asserted in accordance with
the Copyrights, Designs and Patents
Act 1988.

ISBN 978 1 4456 7109 3 (print)
ISBN 978 1 4456 7110 9 (ebook)

British Library Cataloguing in
Publication Data.
A catalogue record for this book is
available from the British Library.

Origination by Amberley Publishing.
Printed in Great Britain.

ABOUT THE AUTHOR

Paul Chrystal was educated at the universities of Hull and Southampton where he took degrees in Classics. He has worked in medical publishing for thirty-five years but now combines this with writing features for national newspapers, as well as advising visitor attractions such as the National Trust's Goddards House, the home of Noel Terry, and York's Chocolate Story. He owned and ran the Knaresborough Bookshop in the High Street for a number of years, appears regularly on BBC local radio, on the PM programme on Radio 4, and on the BBC World Service. He is the author of eighty or so books on a wide range of subjects, including histories of Knaresborough, Harrogate, the Vale of York and other northern places, the Rowntree family, the social history of chocolate, a history of confectionery in Yorkshire and various aspects of classical literature and history. He is married with three children and lives in York.

INTRODUCTION

Historians from Hargrove to Grainge and from Arnold Kellett to Malcolm Neesam have provided excellent histories of Knaresborough, turning up copious amounts of historical information that is now very familiar to many who live here and to others who have visited or studied the town. This book is different because it is a historical journey through Knaresborough, taking in the castle, the High Street, Market Place, industry, poverty, pubs and the river. Mother Shipton and Blind Jack are in there too. It fits in your pocket so it can easily be carried around with you on your tour.

KEY

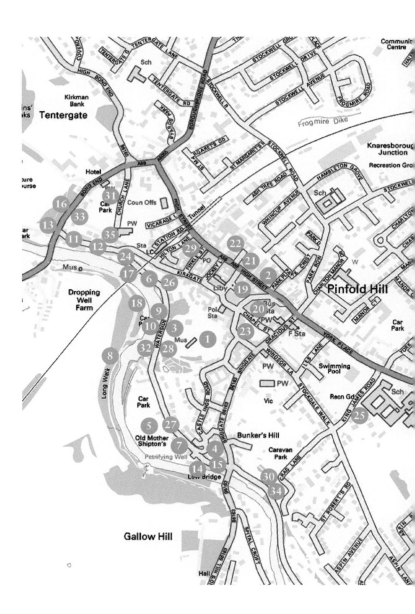

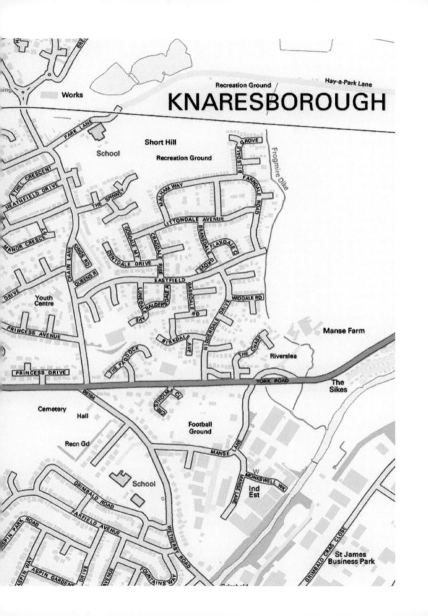

KNARESBOROUGH

Hay-a-Park Lane

Recreation Ground

Works

Frogmire Dike

PARK LANE

GROVE

Short Hill

School

DALESIDE

Recreation Ground

FAIRDALE ROAD

ETHEL CRESCENT

HEATHFIELD DRIVE

THE SPINNEY

HACKFALL WAY

LITTONDALE AVENUE

MANOR CRESC

GENTDALE DRIVE

COCKDALE RISE

CHAGDALE RISE

BRANSDALE

FLAXDALE C

BOWD

CHAIN LANE

KINGS RD

QUEENS R

EASTFIELD

LUNEDALE

FAIRDALE RD

WIDDALE RD

DRIVE

Youth Centre

NIDDERDALE DRIVE

Manse Farm

AVE

BAULDERS DALE

THE CHASE

PRINCESS AVENUE

BIRKDALE

AVE

Riverslea

THE PADDOCK

PRINCESS DRIVE

YORK ROAD

The Sikes

CR

STHOLME CT

Cemetery

Hall

Football Ground

MANSE LANE

Recn Gd

MONKSWELL WAY

MANSE LANE

Ind Est

GRIMBALD ROAD

School

ASPIN PARK ROAD

FARFIELD AVENUE

WETHERBY ROAD

GRIMBALD CRAG CLOSE

ASPIN WAY

ASPIN GARDENS

AVENUE

FOUNTAINS WAY

St James Business Park

THE Saturday Magazine.

Nº 100.   JANUARY   25TH, 1834.   { PRICE ONE PENNY.

UNDER THE DIRECTION OF THE COMMITTEE OF GENERAL LITERATURE AND EDUCATION, APPOINTED BY THE SOCIETY FOR PROMOTING CHRISTIAN KNOWLEDGE.

KNARESBOROUGH, YORKSHIRE.

1. KNARESBOROUGH CASTLE

Knaresborough Castle has its origins in the fortified settlement or burg, which was referred to when the Angles named this place Knarresburg. Strategically placed on rocky ground towering over the Nidd some 120 feet below, the fort was developed as a castle by the Normans, traditionally under Serlo de Burgh, who had fought with William at Hastings. In 1130 Henry I authorised Serlo's nephew, Eustace Fitz-John, to develop the castle, and soon this was a base for hunting wild boar and deer.

The *Chronicle of John de Brompton* tells us that the four knights who murdered the Archbishop Thomas Becket in Canterbury Cathedral on 29 December 1170 fled north and took refuge in Knaresborough Castle – their leader, Hugh de Morville, was constable of the castle.

The chronicle adds that the castle dogs declined to eat the scraps that the four murderers threw from the table.

In 1205 King John appointed Brian de Lisle to extend and strengthen the castle until it became one of the most important military and financial centres in the north, a base from which he could control rebellious barons. He authorised the digging out of a huge dry moat, which started in 1204, and the production of quarrels or crossbow bolts in the castle forges.

King John's castle was completely rebuilt for Piers Gaveston by Edward II between 1307 and 1312, making it a fine residence as well as a stronghold with a dozen towers and a great keep – the total cost was the impressive sum of £2,174.

Following the defeat at Bannockburn, Edward II had to contend with rebellions in England. On 5 October 1317 a rebel knight, John de Lilleburn, took Knaresborough Castle and held it until 29 January 1318, when it was recaptured by the king's forces. Later that year it proved too strong for the Scots to take. From 1328 the castle became the occasional residence of Edward III and Queen Philippa, and also their sons, the Black Prince and John of Gaunt. In 1372 Edward granted the castle and honour of Knaresborough to John of Gaunt, Duke of Lancaster, since which time it has been part of the duchy and, therefore, belongs to the Queen. In Tudor times it was greatly admired by John Leland, who, in 1540, noted that, 'The Castel standeth magnificently and strongley on a Rok.'

The ruins we see today are from Edward II's castle, reduced to this state by Oliver Cromwell's Parliamentarians, not as a result of warfare, but by slighting – the systematic dismantling of Royalist castles – which was carried out here in 1648. Knaresborough Castle had been taken by the Parliamentarians in December 1644. Little remains to remind us of its original splendour except the barbican gate, the keep, and the one thing Cromwell could not destroy, the magnificent panoramic view of the Nidd Gorge.

2. EUGENE ARAM'S SCHOOL IN WHITE HORSE YARD – NOW PARK PLACE

Born at Ramsgill in Nidderdale in 1704, Aram moved to Knaresborough in 1734 and opened a school at the top of High Street in White Horse Yard (now Park Place). A self-educated scholar and linguist, he became involved in a fraudulent scheme with a flax dresser, Richard Houseman, and a young shoemaker, Daniel Clark. On 7 February 1744, Clark disappeared and it was assumed he had absconded with the defrauded valuables. Soon afterwards, Aram paid off his debts and left Knaresborough. In August 1758 a skeleton was discovered buried on Thistle Hill. Houseman, accused of Clark's murder, denied that the bones were Clark's and eventually confessed that he was buried in St Robert's Cave, where he had seen Aram strike Clark down. Traced to King's Lynn, the schoolmaster was arrested and imprisoned in York Castle. In spite of his learned defence speech, he was found guilty at York Assizes and, on 6 August 1759, condemned to be hanged in York, and later hung on the gibbet in Knaresborough, just beyond the Mother Shipton Inn. Two writers made Eugene Aram well known to Victorians: Thomas Hood in *The Dream of Eugene Aram*, which vividly describes his guilty conscience, and Bulwer Lytton in a fanciful novel *Eugene Aram*, which attempts to exonerate him.

3. FIRING THE ROYAL SALUTE

This 24-pounder muzzle-loader canon was captured at Sebastopol during the Crimean War and presented to Knaresborough in 1857; ironically, demand for metal claimed it during the Second World War. This photograph shows a salute being fired to mark the Coronation of George V in June 1911, a few yards to the left of the war memorial.

4. THE CHAPEL OF OUR LADY OF THE CRAG, OR ST ROBERT'S CHAPEL

Often mistakenly called 'St Robert's Chapel' because of confusion with St Robert's Cave, also in the rock face but nearly a mile further down the river, the chapel was cut out of the crag near Low Bridge by John the Mason in 1408 and is reputedly the third oldest wayside shrine in Britain. At 10 feet 6 inches long, 9 feet wide and 7 feet 6 inches high, it was, according to an 1880s guide to Knaresborough, 'elegantly hollowed out of the solid rock: its roof and altar beautifully adorned with Gothic ornaments'. The entrance is guarded by the figure of a knight holding a sword. The knight is 'in the act of drawing his sword to defend the place from the violence of rude intruders'.

Wordsworth visited in 1802, alluding to it in his *Effusion*. Some, including Wordsworth, took this soldier to be one of the Knights Templar. Now officially recognised as a chapel by the Vatican, the 1890 edition of the guide describes the interior: 'Behind the altar is a large niche, where formerly stood an image; and on one side of it a place for the holy water basin. Here also are the figures of three heads designed ... for an emblematical allusion to the order of monks (*Sanctae Trinitatis*) at the once neighbouring priory, by some of whom they were probably cut.' A later image of the Madonna and Child dated from 1916, when the shrine was restored by John Martin. He gave it to Ampleforth Abbey, on whose behalf it is now looked after by the parish of St Mary's, Knaresborough. The current statue was carved by Ian Judd and dedicated in 2000. The chapel is too small to accommodate a congregation, but Mass is occasionally said outside.

MOTHER SHIPTONS CAVE

5. MOTHER SHIPTON'S CAVE

Despite claims by numerous other towns in the UK, this is where we like to think Mother Shipton was born to Agatha during a violent thunderstorm. The Shiptons continue to fascinate to this day, with the comparatively neglected Tobias Shipton celebrated by Middlesbrough poet Bob Beagrie in his 2010 poem 'The Seer Sung Husband'.

6. THE VIADUCT AND THE 'GOZUNDA'

To the west of the station is the 300-foot, four-span (each 56 feet 9 inches wide) viaduct designed by Thomas Grainger Engineering and built by a 270-strong workforce led by George Wilson, a railway contractor. It carries the line over the River Nidd 78 feet below. Disaster struck when it collapsed on 11 March 1848 – almost complete. It took three and a half years to rebuild and eventually opened in 1851 at a cost of £9,803. The picture shows a British Railways inspection taking place in 1960 using the 'Gozunda' (a hydraulically operated rail-mounted viaduct inspection unit to you and me).

7. THE DROPPING WELL, 1959

Lethal-looking icicles festoon the Dropping Well on a freezing winter day in January 1959. One of Britain's oldest tourist attractions, this petrifying well derives its name from the water dropping over a limestone rock into a little pool before joining the Nidd. The earliest known description is by John Leland, the antiquary of Henry VIII. After his visit in around 1538, he wrote of 'a Welle of a wonderful nature, caullid Droping Welle. For out of the great rokkes by it distillith water continually into it ... what thing so ever ys caste in and is touched of this water, growth ynto stone'.

A tourist attraction since 1630, the petrifying well has intrigued visitors with its seemingly magical ability to change everyday objects into stone by depositing layers of calcite. Seven hundred gallons of water flow through every hour and it takes approximately six months to 'petrify' a teddy bear, for example. Today, the well features a highly imaginative array of articles, some of which are in the castle museum. Nowadays the overhang is regularly scraped to prevent collapse, as happened in 1704, 1816 and 1823. Neither Leland nor any other early visitor refers to a nearby cave, later claimed to be the birthplace of the Tudor prophetess Mother Shipton, though the two are now closely associated.

The Dropping Well estate, covering 12 acres, with the Long Walk and its beautiful views of Knaresborough across the river, was owned by the Slingsby family until 1916, when it was sold off by auction. The Long Walk was used by Madame Doreen, palmist and clairvoyant, who gave special consultations by appointment. It was bought in 1986 by a company then headed by Frank McBratney and Paul Daniels, and its name was changed to Mother Shipton's Cave Ltd.

8. THE HUT, LONG WALK

This was used by Madame Doreen, palmist and clairvoyant, who gave special consultations by appointment. The Long Walk describes the riverside avenue with its fine views of the town, which leads from High Bridge to the Dropping Well. This was much used in the days when 'Knaresborough Spa' still referred to the town itself, and later when Harrogate had taken over as the spa and visitors came to Knaresborough for recreation as part of 'the cure'. Daniel Defoe records walking along here in 1717. The Long Walk was later landscaped by Sir Henry Slingsby in around 1739.

9. BOATING ON THE NIDD

Boating is still a major attraction on the Nidd today. This photograph shows Edwardian boaters near the boathouses at High Bridge. William Bluett was the first to let boats here, followed by Richard Sturdy under the castle and Charles Blenkhorn. The Venerable Bede talks of a synod held near the Nidd in AD 706, during the reign of King Osred. In the first year of Osred's reign Bertwald, Archbishop of Canterbury and primate of nearly the whole of Britain, came up from the south to judge Wilfred. The result was the reinstating of Wilfred, Bishop of Northumbria and Hexham, as requested by Pope John VI.

10. PENSIVE LADY ON *MARIGOLD*

The *Marigold* houseboat was owned by the O'Reilly sisters and spent most of its time as an Edwardian café restaurant moored between Sturdy's and Castle Mill. It played a key role in the annual Water Carnivals as the venue for a brass band; unfortunately it sank, derelict, in 1920. The O'Reilly sisters also ran the Moat Café. *Marigold* housed a stylish restaurant, serving food on the upper deck. Sometimes she sailed out on the river, especially during the Water Carnival. The riverside Marigold Café preserves the old name.

11. STURDY & SON BOATBUILDERS

The River Nidd has always been central to Knaresborough's tourism. This shows some of the boats built and hired out by Sturdy & Son (140 to Blenkhorn's ninety). Founded by Richard Sturdy (1837–1913) around 1850, the firm bought and expanded the boat business previously run by a Mr Bluett. Sturdy's was subsequently taken over by Bill Henry and then sold to Harrogate Council in 1965.

Knaresborough Castle

12. STURDY'S BOATS

Sturdy's built the boats they hired out. This 1914 photograph shows Frank Sturdy (son of the founder, Richard) at work – Frank did his apprenticeship in York. At this time Frank had taken on George Smith, an apprentice aged twelve.

13. HIGH BRIDGE

Originally called Danyell Bridge, it was widened in 1773 and then again in 1924 in response to the growing traffic on what is now the A59 Harrogate road. This 1938 picture shows an early traffic policeman, the High Bridge Private Hotel (opened in 1906), the New Century Dining Rooms (1900) and the timbered World's End pub in the distance. All three establishments were owned by Charles Blenkhorn, who also competed with Richard Sturdy in the boating business.

14. RUG WORKS

Knaresborough's main industry was linen, but this shows the Knaresborough rug works (Holgates) as painted by Joseph Baker Fountain (1907–92) with fleeces being washed and drying in the garden. Pigot & Co.'s *Royal, National and Commercial* (1841), tells us that the companies based at Low Bridge in the mid-nineteenth century were J. Clapham, William Clapham & Co. (both of whom specialised in sheep skin), and William Hartley with Jacob Edmondson in Market Place. Clapham's is next to the gasworks in a building that was formerly a soap factory run by Joe Clough.

The manufacture of linen was a cottage industry in Knaresborough dating from the thirteenth century and reflected the spread of a rural cloth industry throughout Yorkshire to compete with the urban-centred industries at York and Beverley. Water-powered fulling mills came from this development and were built for the thickening and felting of cloth. Before the mills, cloth had been fulled by walking (trampling) on it; the mills were, therefore, called walking mills while the fuller was a walker, hence the common surname. The first fulling mill at Knaresborough was mentioned in 1284 – it was on the north bank of the Nidd above the High Bridge. It crops up again in the sixteenth century when it is described as being in Walkmyln Lonnying (lane) on the Coghill (Conyngham) Hall estate. This places it near Tentergate, named after the frames on which the cloth was stretched to dry after fulling or dying.

KNARESBORO

15. LOW BRIDGE

Formerly known as March Bridge (which means a boundary), Low Bridge was widened in 1779. The 1856 Holy Trinity Church off Gracious Street dominates the horizon with its 166-foot spire, designed by John Fawcett and costing £3,800 to build. Harker's rug manufacturers is at the far end of the bridge; it is now long gone, although the other buildings over the road in Abbey Road largely survive, one of which is a shop selling doll's houses, models and second-hand books.

Holy Trinity was built as an addition to St John's when the population of Knaresborough grew big enough to merit the formation of another parish with its own parish church. Situated just off Briggate, Holy Trinity has become, with its 166-foot spire, a landmark visible for miles around. Designed by Joseph Fawcett in the modern Early Decorated style, it was built at a cost of £3,800. Consecrated by the Bishop of Ripon, the church opened in 1856. Though the steeple was designed to take a clock and could hold a full peal of eight bells, only one bell materialised – the gift of Basil Woodd of Conyngham Hall (later replaced in 1994 by the bell from Thistle Hill chapel).

16. KNARESBOROUGH ZOO

A popular attraction for many years, this 1969 shot shows the zoo's owner, Edward Milborrow, with Irma the elephant. Irma was something of a film star and shared her home with breeding bears, lions, tigers, llamas, wallabies, penguins and monkeys.

Knaresborough Zoo was established in the grounds of Conyngham Hall in 1965 under Nick Nyoka, who made expeditions to the world's jungles to bring back exotic animals. These included Simba, at the time the biggest lion in captivity. The zoo became a popular tourist attraction, especially when Nyoka demonstrated snake handling (*nyoka* is Swahili for 'snake'). In its heyday the zoo attracted 150,000 visitors each year, 10,000 of these in school parties. However, by 1985 conditions were considered unsatisfactory by Harrogate Borough Council, who refused to renew the licence. A campaign to close the zoo was supported by a visit from Virginia McKenna; others pleaded for its retention, but there was no financial backing and, after an unsuccessful appeal, it closed in November 1986. Nick Nyoka died in 1995. Much of the zoo's land was used for the building of Henshaw's Art and Craft Centre in 1999.

17. KNARESBOROUGH VIADUCT

The viaduct and a train crossing above the frozen River Nidd in 1947. One of the most dramatic incidents in the history of Knaresborough was the collapse of the first railway viaduct across the Nidd just after midday, at 12.15 p.m., on Saturday 11 March 1848. The thunderous roar of falling masonry is said to have lasted five minutes. The foundation stone had been laid amid great rejoicing the previous April by Joseph Dent of Ribston Hall, High Sheriff of Yorkshire. But poor workmanship, shoddy materials and heavy rain led to it crashing into the river when it was almost completed. Tom Collins, later MP for Knaresborough, narrowly missed being crushed, but there was no loss of life except for multitudes of fish killed by the lime in the mortar. Waterside was flooded to a depth of 12 feet and much damage was done, but eventually the viaduct was rebuilt to a design by Thomas Grainger at the joint expense of two railway companies and at a cost of £9,803. The contractors Duckett & Stead finally completed this spectacular structure – 90 feet high, 338 feet long – with four arches of 56 foot spans. It was opened on 1 October 1851. Nicklaus Pevsner deplored the way the railway cut through the heart of the town, but J. B. Priestley admired the way the viaduct reflected in the river and 'added a double beauty to the scene'.

18. BOATING

The River Nidd running through the town, with its delightfully varied views, has long been popular for recreation in boats, and, more recently, canoes and punts. The first known provider of boats was William Bluet, who died in 1850. He was followed by Richard Sturdy of Richmond House, whose landing stage and boathouse were just below the castle. The work, including boatbuilding, was continued during the 1900s by his son, Frank, and a veteran boatman, George Smith. The last boat was built here in around 1927. Sturdy's was originally licensed for 140 boats. A second boatman, Charles Blenkhorn, adjacent to High Bridge, started with ninety boats. Sturdy's was taken over after the war by Billy Henry, who sold it to the council in 1965.

19. 'DOWN AND OUT' AND BLIND JACK

This emotive photograph was taken just before the Second World War and entitled 'Down and Out' – a stark reminder of the poverty that existed at the time. Local legend Blind Jack (really John Metcalf 1717–1810) now occupies a bench nearby, impressively cast in bronze by local artist Barbara Asquith in February 2009. The market cross has something of a chequered history. The circular stone base dates from 1709, added when a new cross was erected. This was replaced in 1824 when a gas engineer, John Malam, donated a gas lamp. The arrival of electricity meant that this was replaced by a hideous transformer and a tall stand, with lamps on three branches. To celebrate the Queen's coronation in 1953 a market cross was reinstated, although this too was not without its detractors. A supposedly fourteenth-century-style cross in a circle now decorates Market Place.

Metcalf was a jack of all trades despite his disability and at various times was musician, drinker, road builder, hunter, cockfight gambler, horse dealer and smuggler. He constructed 180 miles of road, earning £65,000.

19a. BOND END

A family scene from the end of the nineteenth century in cottages at Bond End near the World's End pub; through various slum clearance programmes these and similar dwellings are long gone. The box on the left contained table jelly. Bond End is the name for the once-distinct community at the bottom of High Street. The name originates from the fact that the boundary of the outer area in which serfs or bondsmen once lived was situated here. Above and beyond Bond End was the free burg of Knaresborough itself, whose inhabitants were in 1310 granted the various freedoms enjoyed by burgesses. In 2011, buildings at the junction with High Street were demolished and replaced with new housing.

20. WARSHIP WEEK, 1942

WAAFs processioning into the Market Place from the High Street during Warship Week in March 1942; the officer taking the salute was Rear Admiral L. Forbes-Sempill. Boots is still there in the building on the right. Knaresborough Synagogue was at the exit to Synagogue Lane, at the rear of Market Place, where the thirteenth-century Jewish community worshipped. The community was probably dissolved in 1275 just before all Jews were expelled from the country in 1290 by Edward I.

Kearton

High St., Knaresbro, Market Day

21. HIGH STREET DONKEYS

Around 1905, when this photograph was taken, it was not unusual to see livestock such as geese (shod as they came from afar), donkeys, cattle and sheep in the High Street on Wednesdays as part of the market. A purpose-built livestock market opened in 1907. Knaresborough has a long association with donkeys thanks to Donkey Dave Allott – the Donkeyman – a familiar figure in the town for many years with his riverside donkey rides and charity donkey derbys.

C B Southwell Chemist Knaresbro

22. KNARESBOROUGH ROCK SOLD HERE

Betty and Mary Fisher are shown here outside their sweetshop and café at No. 45 High Street. They had moved from London in 1931 and later moved to smaller premises at No. 25 Castlegate. One of their specialties was Knaresborough rock. The property has retained much of its original character and later became the toy and gift shop Indigo.

23. MORRISON'S ANTIQUES

This photograph shows Miss Elizabeth Morrison outside her antiques shop, established in the 1860s at No. 28 Cheapside. The drawing shows the original shop in Market Place in what is now the Blind Jack pub. In the 1960s Miss Morrison sold the business to Vollans the photographers, established in 1949, who still trades from the premises.

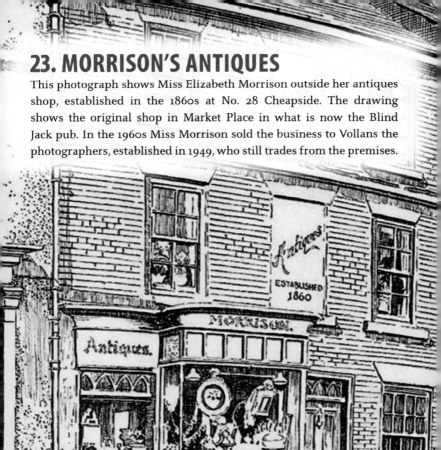

24. MANOR COTTAGE THATCHERS IN WATER BAG BANK

The only surviving thatched dwelling in Knaresborough is also one of its oldest, built as it was in Tudor times. Sadly the thatching and some of the sixteenth-century beams were completely destroyed in an arson attack in April 2009 and £300,000 worth of damage was inflicted on the Grade I-listed building, which has now been repaired. The cottage is at the foot of Water Bag Bank, named after the leather water bags carried up to the town full of water from the sewage-filled Nidd on mules to assist the women who did the job for a halfpenny a trip. At the lower end of Kirkgate, where it goes down to the Nidd, it is the only fully cobbled street in the town. This was, however, never Knaresborough's only source of water.

25. DESIGN AND TECHNOLOGY, 1952 STYLE

A woodwork class at St James's School in 1952. In the beginning discipline was strict, and the master was to see that his boys did not come to school 'uncombed, unwashed, ragged or slovenly'. He was to 'severely punish swearing, lying, picking [pockets], stealing, fighting, quarrelling, wanton speech, uncleane behaviour and such like'. Parents had to supply 'candles for the winter', and a bow and arrows for the games period as practice

for war. There was great emphasis on grammar, both in Latin and English, on the catechism, the Creed and the psalms. In later years, the school motto was taken from Psalm 116: '*Quid retribuam Domino?*' ('What shall I give back to the Lord?'). Anyone 'unapte to learne' after a year was expelled. There was zero tolerance on absenteeism too: 'he shall be utterly expelled' unless caused by illness. School started at 6 a.m. in the summer and 7 a.m. in the winter, with an assembly in which the boys recited, on their knees, not just any old psalm but the longest of them all, Psalm 119 (176 verses), the Creed, the Lord's Prayer and the catechism. After year one they had to converse in Latin at all times, including playtime.

26. EDWARD VII

His coronation in 1902 was commemorated by the joiner and undertaker Benjamin Woodward, who named the house he built that year, No. 45 Kirkgate, Coronation Cottage and added the coloured plaque of the king, which can still be seen today.

Mother Shipton was a wise woman and knew a good place. Come and try

Knaresborough

27. MOTHER SHIPTON

Born in 1488 (predating Nostradamus by fifteen years) in a cave next to the River Nidd, the legendary Mother Shipton (nee Ursula Southeil) is synonymous with Knaresborough and with the art of prophecy. Afflicted by what was probably scoliosis and variously branded a witch and the Devil's daughter, her predictions have included the demise of Cardinal Wolsey, the Gunpowder Plot, the Great Fire of London, her own death, and, as yet unsuccessfully, the end of the world (1881 and 1991). The first account of her did not appear until 1641. This describes how, when living in York, she had predicted that the disgraced Cardinal Wolsey, who planned to be enthroned as archbishop in 1530, would see York, but never reach the city. Wolsey got as far as Cawood Castle, and from the tower saw York Minster in the distance, vowing he would have Mother Shipton burnt as a witch. But he was arrested on a charge of high treason and died on the journey south. This first printed version of the prophecies spread the fame of Mother Shipton throughout England. In 1667, a fictionalised account of her by Richard Head stated she had been born (after her mother had been seduced by the devil in disguise) at Knaresborough, 'near the Dropping Well'. Head's publication contains the first of many fabricated prophecies attributed to Mother Shipton, all written after the events (e.g. the defeat of the Spanish Armada). Forgeries were taken a stage further by the Brighton bookseller Charles Hindley, who in 1873 confessed that he had made up prophecies about modern inventions and one that had caused much alarm: 'Then the world to an end shall come; In eighteen hundred and eighty one.'

William Grainge noted that in 1848, when the viaduct collapsed, locals had started saying that Mother Shipton had always predicted that 't' big brig across t' Nidd should tummle doon twice, an' stand fer ivver when built a third time' – a garbled version of which still survives, linked with the end of the world.

Until around 1908, a cottage near Low Bridge was regularly visited as the birthplace of Mother Shipton. The cave near the Dropping Well, though associated with her from Victorian times, was not publicised as the actual birthplace until around 1918. Outside Knaresborough the prophetess became a figure of folklore. For 200 years or so, she was familiar as a puppet who smoked a real pipe. A moth has been named after her: *callistege mi*, which apparently bears a profile of a hag's head on each wing. She became a popular character in pantomime, her part played by men including David Garrick in 1759, making her the first real pantomime dame. By 1770, at Covent Garden, Mother Shipton's spectacular transformation scenes also made her the first fairy godmother.

28. BLIND JACK

Blind Jack was the nickname of John Metcalf, who was born in 1717 in a cottage (demolished in around 1768) near the parish church and was a true jack of all trades. He went to school aged four, but at the age of six was afflicted by smallpox, which left him completely blind. An intelligent boy with prodigious determination and energy, he led an active life of tree climbing, swimming, hunting and gambling. At fifteen he was appointed fiddler at the Queen's Head in High Harrogate. He later earned money as a guide, especially at night time, and eloped with Dolly Benson, daughter of the landlord of the Royal Oak (later the Granby). In 1745 he marched as a musician to Scotland, leading Captain Thornton's 'Yorkshire Blues' to fight Bonnie Prince Charlie's rebels.

Blind Jack is best known for his work as a pioneer of road building. His extensive travels and the stagecoach he ran between York and Knaresborough had acquainted him with the appalling state of English roads. Soon after a new Turnpike Act in 1752, he obtained a contract for building (with his gang of workmen) a 3-mile stretch of road between Ferrensby and Minskip. Then he built part of the road from Knaresborough to Harrogate, including a bridge over the Starbeck, and went on to complete around 180 miles of road in Yorkshire, Lancashire and Derbyshire. The specially constructed viameter he used to measure his roads can be seen in the Courthouse Museum. Following Dolly's death in 1778, he went to live with his married daughter in Spofforth. Here, after many active years in business and as a violin player, he died in 1810, leaving behind four children, twenty grandchildren and ninety great- and great-great grandchildren. A tombstone in Spofforth churchyard pays tribute to the remarkable achievements of 'Blind Jack of Knaresborough', and, as noted, he was commemorated with a bronze statue by Barbara Asquith in Knaresborough Market Place in 2009.

29. OLD OAK ROOM, CROWN HOTEL

A wonderful photograph from the early 1900s showing the wood-panelled room inside this pub with a customer enjoying a quiet read; the only thing missing is a pint of ale. Baines Directory of 1822 lists thirty-nine other pubs and hotels in Knaresborough. Around this time the Crown boasted an impressive external clock, was owned by Tetley's, and the landlord was a W. Broadley.

30. THE HALF MOON

Knaresborough was once renowned for its extraordinary number of inns – seventy-four have been noted during the eighteenth and nineteenth centuries. These did good trade around market day and provided accommodation for spa visitors and travellers, as well as social centres for residents, particularly those keen on cockfighting. Many inns referred to in early documents no longer survive. They included, for example, the Barrel, the Elephant & Castle, the Star Inn, two called the White Horse, and the Shoulder of Mutton. Others have been rebuilt, such as the World's End (1898), or replaced by a modern building on the same site, such as the Ivy Cottage. Some, however, remained almost unchanged over the centuries, in particular the Old Royal Oak, the Mother Shipton (once called the Dropping Well), the Half Moon, the Crown, the Hart's Horn, the Marquis of Granby, the Commercial (once called the Borough Bailiff), the George & Dragon, and the Yorkshire Lass (formerly the George Hotel and the Murray Arms).

WILLIAM. W
LICENSED
ALE &
NOT TO BE CONSU
TOBACCO

31. MRS WHEELHOUSE AND FLORENCE

This shop in Church Lane around 1898 is an early off-licence, selling as it does ale and porter as well as the usual tobacco, chocolate and sweets. The picture shows Mrs Wheelhouse and daughter Florence.

32. RIVERSIDE COTTAGES

Taken around 1909 with the castle towering in the background, this scene, maid aside, remains much the same 100 or so years later.

33. THE WORLD'S END

The name World's End is usually, but not always, associated with the execution of Charles I. This is the World's End as it was around 1898. The licensee, Charles Blenkhorn, also ran a pleasure boat business near High Bridge, as the sign shows. This pub replaced the original tavern on the site. Blenkhorn was also town postmaster and his sister was postmistress. At one time the pub sign is said to have depicted an earthquake with a bus falling into a river.

34. ABBEY ROAD ON WASHING DAY

This view shows the Star Inn on the left and Horsman's, the rug maker, on the right of Abbey Road. This once led to the friary (the Trinitarian House of St Robert) that stood just below the Chapel of our Lady of the Crag. The original priory had been destroyed in 1318 by the armies of Robert Bruce but was rebuilt by Edward III. In 1366 Archbishop Thoresby decreed 'that in future the cloister and dormitory should be kept free from the invasion of secular persons, and especially women of doubtful character, both day and night'. Robert Ashton, one of the organisers of the Pilgrimage of Grace, was a friar here in the 1530s. The washing, part of the pub and Horsman's are no more, but much else remains the same.

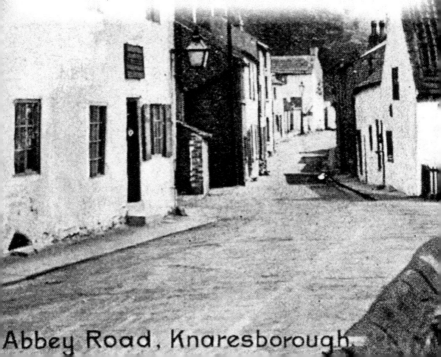

Abbey Road, Knaresborough.

The Lawn Mother Shipton Inn

35. FEEDING THE CHICKENS IN THE GARDEN, DROPPING WELL INN

The inn was part of the Slingsby estate. Sir Charles Slingsby was perhaps the most famous member of the family; he died tragically on a ferry on the River Ure at Newby Hall while out hunting in 1869 along with six other men and eight horses. His sister, Emma Louisa, dedicated a tomb to Sir Charles in the Slingsby Chapel in the parish church of St John the Baptist.

CHEAPSIDE

'Cheap' means 'market' and signifies that this street bordered onto the market. The shop on the near right is F. Wade with the boy avidly looking at postcards in the window. Further down on the right the sign tells us that the shop there sells cycle tyres. Neat cottages have replaced the shops. The entrance to Holy Trinity Church is at the end of the road on Gracious Street.

ENGLAND'S UNIQUE WATER PAGEANT

Knaresborough Water Carnival, a magnificent spectacle that really came to life after nightfall when Brock's provided a fantastic firework display. The viaduct was transformed into Niagara Falls (costing £58 in 1903). Don Pedro crossing the river by tightrope, a fairy castle, the Eiffel Tower, the houseboat (the *Marigold*) with forty dancers and a brass band, and a spotlight picking out notable local characters such as Mother Shipton completed the scene.

KNARESBOROUGH HISTORY TIMELINE

c. 10,000 BC Nidd Gorge formed following Great Ice Age

500 BC Ancient Britons (Brigantes) give a Celtic name to the River Nidd

AD 74 Romans finally defeat Brigantes, build Isurium Brigantum

AD 410 Angles build the fortified settlement of Knarresburg

AD 705 Synod of Nidd, recorded by St Bede

AD 867 First Vikings settle here, following their capture of York

1066 Norman settlement. Serlo de Burgh is the first lord of Knaresborough

1070 Harrying of the North – brutal Norman suppression. Castle started

1086 Domesday Book notes 'Chenaresburgh' with villages and land for twenty-four ploughs

1114 Knaresborough parish church granted by Henry I to Nostell Priory

1133 Eustace Fitz-John sends bread to starving monks building fountains

1167 Forest of Knaresborough established as a royal hunting ground

1170 Becket's four murderers, led by Hugh de Moreville, flee to the castle

1206 First visit by King John. First reference to Knaresborough Market

1210 First known Royal Maundy. King John gives alms to thirteen paupers here

1216 King John visits St Robert in his riverside hermitage, grants him land

1257 Priory of St Robert. Charter from John's son, Richard Plantagenet

1300 Edward I, staying at castle, visits St Robert's tomb

1310 Knaresborough granted its first known charter by Edward II

1312 Castle rebuilt for Piers Gaveston (twelve towers and a keep)

1314 Edward II orders Knaresborough men to march to Bannockburn

1317 Castle taken by rebel knight John de Lilleburn

1318 Castle recaptured. Scots raid town, burn church and 140 houses

1328 Edward III and Queen Philippa, newly married, visit Knaresborough

1331 Queen Philippa granted the Honour of Knaresborough by Edward III

1343 Parish church restored and reconsecrated under Queen Philippa

1349 The Black Death reaches Knaresborough

1372 John of Gaunt, Duke of Lancaster, made Lord of Knaresborough

1399 Richard II is kept prisoner in Knaresborough Castle before his death at Pontefract

1408 Chapel of Our Lady of the Crag excavated by John the Mason

1488 Birth of Mother Shipton, according to legend

1451 Sir William Plumpton secretly marries Joan Wintringham

1461 Battle of Towton in the War of the Roses. Many Knaresborough men killed

1520 Miniature 'candle-snuffer' spire added to church

1536 Pilgrimage of Grace. Protests against Henry VIII's reforms

1540 Leland, Henry VIII's antiquary, praises castle, market, Dropping Well

1553 Knaresborough returns its first two Members of Parliament

1561 Parish register started. Protestant service firmly established

1588 Guy Fawkes moves to Scotton. Converted to Catholicism

1600 Death of Francis Slingsby. Tomb in Slingsby Chapel

1605 Gunpowder Plot, Guy Fawkes fails to destroy King James

1616 King James's Grammar School founded by Revd Dr Robert Chaloner

1626 Dr Edmund Deane's *Spadacrene Anglica* promotes Knaresborough

1638 Charity for giving bread to the poor, first of many

1641 First account of Mother Shipton's prediction of Wolsey's downfall

1642 Sir Henry Slingsby secures castle for Charles I

1644 Battle of Marston Moor. Siege of Knaresborough Castle

1648 Castle systematically demolished. Cromwell stays in Knaresborough

1658 Sir Harry Slingsby beheaded on Tower Hill and buried in the parish church

1660 Restoration of Charles II

1666 George Fox visits Scotton and Knaresborough

1688 Sir Henry Goodricke proclaims the Prince of Orange as William III

1697 Independents' Barn chapel opens. Celia Fiennes in Knaresborough

1717 Daniel Defoe stays in Knaresborough. Birth of Blind Jack

1720 The oldest chemist's shop in England opens in the Market Place

1732 Blind Jack appointed fiddler for spa visitors at Harrogate inns

1734 Eugene Aram starts school in White Horse Yard, High Street

1735 Revd Thomas Collins, vicar of Knaresborough until 1788

1737 Knaresborough's first workhouse built near the parish church

1739 Sir Henry Slingsby lays out the Long Walk by the Dropping Well

1741 King James's Grammar School rebuilt on same site

1742 First visits by John Wesley – Methodist meetings

1744 Linen industry flourishing. Disappearance of Daniel Clark

1745 Yorkshire Blues formed here, march to fight rebels in Scotland

1759 Eugene Aram hanged in York for the murder of Daniel Clark

1764 Act of Parliament authorises a water pump on the Nidd

1765 Thomas Richardson's Charity School opens. Blind Jack building roads

1768 Knaresborough House, High Street, built for the Collins family

1770 House in the Rock started by a poor linen weaver, Thomas Hill

1774 First known fire engine. Peal of eight bells in parish church

1785 Walton's linen manufacturers established. Sunday schools start

1795 First known public library in Knaresborough

1791 Castle Mill built for cotton (later adapted for Walton's linen)

1796 Conyngham Hall built on site of Tudor Coghill House

1803 Free Dispensary of Medicine started by Dr Peter Murray, Castle Ings

1810 Death of Blind Jack at Spofforth, where he is buried

1814 Castle Boys School opens as Church of England National School

1815 Methodist chapel opens off Gracious Street. Cricket club founded

1818 Death of Ely Hargrove, local historian, aged seventy-seven

1822 Revival of Knaresborough Spa at Starbeck

1823 Act of Parliament authorises Improvement Commissioners to run town

1824 Gasworks constructed by John Malam. First street lamps

1825 Birth of William Stubbs, later medieval historian, Bishop of Oxford

1831 St Mary's Catholic Church built at Bond End

1837 Castle Girls School opens opposite Castle Boys School

1838 Queen Victoria appoints Walton's suppliers of all royal linen

1843 Literary and Scientific Institution established

1848 Collapse into Nidd of almost-completed railway viaduct

1849 Second outbreak of cholera, thirty-eight deaths. Dinsdale's grocers established

1851 Viaduct rebuilt. Railway line to Starbeck opens

1853 New Free Dispensary built in Castle Yard in memory of Revd A. Cheap

1854 Opening of the Primitive Methodist chapel, off Briggate

1856 Holy Trinity Church completed, with 166-foot spire

1857 First issue of *Knaresborough Household Almanack*

1858 New workhouse in Stockwell Road, later Knaresborough Hospital

1862 Town Hall built on site of Borough Courthouse

1863 *Knaresborough Post* first published

1865 Congregationalist chapel built, Windsor Lane. Castle Yard Riots

1867 Reform bill reduces Knaresborough's two MPs to one

1868 New Wesleyan Methodist chapel, Gracious Street

1869 Sir Charles Slingsby drowned in the Ure in a hunting accident

1872 Restoration of parish church of St John's. Oddfellows Hall opened

1876 Knaresborough Cemetery opened

1885 Knaresborough loses right to elect an MP

1887 Queen Victoria's Golden Jubilee. Knaresborough's 'Rejoicings'

1894 Knaresborough Urban District Council established. First chairman Basil T. Woodd

1895 Richardson's School amalgamates with King James's Grammar School

1898 Kitching's timber merchants established in Knaresborough

1900 Blenkhorn's New Century Dining Rooms, High Bridge

1901 Grammar School moves to York Road, opened by Lord Harewood

1903 Sellars leather factory burnt down. Chamber of Trade founded

1904 Opening of Park Grove Methodist Church

1907 Cattle market moves from High Street

1910 Crowded Market Place to hear proclamation of George V

1911 Population of Knaresborough 5,315 (Harrogate 33,703)

1913 Public electric lighting introduced

1914 Outbreak of First World War; hundreds of men volunteer

1915 Council School moves from Gracious Street to Stockwell Road

1916 Slingsby estate broken up and sold by public auction

1918 End of war. Knaresborough has lost 156 men killed in action

1922 A. S. (Sam) Robinson appointed head of King James's Grammar School

1924 Sir Harold Mackintosh tenant of Conyngham Hall (until 1942)

1926 Public tennis courts opened in castle grounds

1929 Fysche Hall playing fields opened by Lady Evelyn Collins

1931 Moat Gardens (later Bebra Gardens) opened near castle

1942 Warship Week: Knaresborough greatest savings per head in country

1945 End of war. Knaresborough has lost fifty-four killed

1946 Conyngham Hall and grounds bought by Urban District Council

1947 Philip Inman of Charing Cross Hospital, Lord Inman
of Knaresborough

1950 Water Carnival revived. Population of Knaresborough 8,590

1951 KUDC buys Knaresborough House for council offices

1953 Celebration of Coronation of Elizabeth II. New Market
Cross dedicated

1960 Friendship and Leisure Centre opened in Market Place

1962 Knaresborough Players founded, later move to Frazer Theatre

1965 Knaresborough Zoo opens. (Closed in 1986)

1966 First Bed Race. 350th Anniversary of King James's Grammar School

1968 First Boxing Day Tug of War: Half Moon v. Mother Shipton's

1969 Town twinning. Albert Holch chairman of council for sixth time

1971 King James's School starts as eleven to eighteen comprehensive on
same site

1972 Duchess of Kent officially opens King James's School. Pageant

1973 Churchyard of St John's cleared and landscaped

1974 Knaresborough Town Council replaces KUDC. First town mayor

1975 Methodist church rebuilt in Gracious Street

1977 Courthouse Museum opened. Queen drives through Knaresborough

1983 First fun run held by King James's School

1984 Collins Court opened by Lady Elizabeth Collins

1985 Arnold Kellett establishes that first known Royal Maundy in Knaresborough

1986 Hewitson Court opened in memory of Councillor P. W. Hewitson

1988 Town crier (Sid Bradley) appointed. First Edwardian Christmas fair

1989 Knaresborough Community church starts

1990 Opening, after long campaign, of Knaresborough Swimming Pool

1993 Chamber of Trade's first Spring Fair

1996 First Knaresborough Festival of Poetry, Arts and Music (later FEVA)

1998 Duke of Edinburgh shown around Knaresborough, including views of castle

1999 Henshaw's Arts and Crafts Centre opens

2000 New millennium opens: church bells, fireworks, Millennium Pageant

2001 George A. Moore and Arnold Kellett made Freemen of Knaresborough

2002 Market Place reordered and partly pedestrianised

2003 King James's wins both Teacher of the Year (Paul Keogh) and *Mastermind* (Andy Page, former pupil)

2004 Lottery win of just under £6 million by John and Alex Dyer, stewards of Knaresborough Working Men's Club. Age Concern receives Queen's Award for Voluntary Service.

2005 Friends of Bebra Gardens founded

2006 Knaresborough Castle mosaic by Julie Cope

2007 Civic Society's various historical plaques

2008 Miss Jacob-Smith Park opened

2009 Blind Jack statue by Barbara Asquith installed in Market Place. Viaduct Terrace opened

2010 800th Anniversary of Knaresborough Royal Maundy celebrated here

2014 Tour de France speeds through Knaresborough

FURTHER READING

Anonymous, *A Week at Harrogate*, 1913.

Anonymous, *Mother Shipton*, N.D.

Calvert, M., *History of Knaresborough*, 1844.

Chrystal, P.,

A Children's History of Harrogate & Knaresborough, 2011

Knaresborough Through Time, 2010

North York Moors Through Time

Tadcaster Through Time

The Vale of York Through Time

A–Z Knaresborough History (2004, revised 2011)

Chocolate: A History of the Chocolate Industry in Britain, 2011

A History of Chocolate in York, 2011

Secret Knaresborough, 2014

Secret Harrogate, 2015

Harrogate History Tour, 2016

Harrogate Pubs, including Knaresborough, 2016

Deane, E., *Spadacrene Anglica*, 1626.

French, J. The Yorkshire Spaw, 1652.

Floyer, Sir J., *History of Cold Bathing*, 1706.

Grainge, W., *Nidderdale*, 1863.

Grainge, W., *Historical and Descriptive Account of Knaresborough*, 1865.

Gent, T., *Life of St. Robert*, ND.

Hargrove, E., *History of Knaresborough*, 1832.

Hargrove, E., *Ancient Customs of the Forest of Knaresborough*, 1808.

Hutton, W. H., *Life of Bishop Stubbs*, 1906.

Kellet, A., *The Knaresborough Story*, 1972 (new edition 1990)

    The Gracious Street Story, 1975)

    The Queen's Church, 1978

    Knaresborough in Old Picture Postcards, 1984 (new edition 1996)

    Exploring Knaresborough, (1985)

    Scotton and its Methodist Chapel, (1985)

    'King John in Knaresborough: the First Known Royal Maundy' (*Yorkshire Archaeological Journal* offprint, 1990)

    Companion to St John's, 1990

    Historic Knaresborough, 1991

    Knaresborough: Archive Photographs, 1995 (new edition 2003)

    Mother Shipton: Witch and Prophetess, 2002

    King James's School, Knaresborough: 1616–2003, 2003

    A–Z Knaresborough History, 2004 (revised 2011)

    Blind Jack of Knaresborough, 2008

Lewis, D., *Beauties of Harrogate and Knaresborough*, 1798.

Metcalf, J., *Autobiography*, 1795.

Slingsby, Sir H., *Memoirs*: Ed. Sir Walter Scott, 1806.

Speight, H., *Nidderdale*, 1894.

Stubbs, B. P., *Genealogical History of his Family*, 1915.

Stanhope, M., Newes out of Yorkshire, 1626.

Stanhope, M., *Cures without Care*, 1632.

Watson, E. R., *Eugene Aram*, 1913.

Wheater, W., *Knaresburgh and its Rulers,* 1907

House Boat Café, Knaresborough.

Gallon Steps, Knaresborough.